IFEOMA ONYEFULU was brought up in eastern Nigeria.
After completing a business management course in London, she trained as a photographer.
Her internationally-acclaimed photography has been described by Books for Keeps
as 'stepping from a darkened room straight into noon sunshine'.

A is for Africa, her first book for Frances Lincoln, was praised by Publishers Weekly for its
'incisive, sophisticated view of her homeland's rich heritage'. The book was selected
as one of Child Education's best information books of 1993 and Junior Education's Best Books
of 1994, and was followed by *Emeka's Gift: An African Counting Story.* Her next book,
One Big Family: Sharing Life in an African Village, was chosen as a 1997 Notable Book for Children
by the American Library Association and as a Notable Children's Trade Book in the Field of
Social Studies by the National Council for Social Studies and the Children's Book Council
in America. In 1997 *Chidi Only Likes Blue: An African Book of Colours* won a Scientific American
Young Readers Book Award. *My Grandfather is a Magician,* published in 1998,
describes the work and wisdom of a traditional African healer.
Her latest books are *Ebele's Favourite: A Book of African Games, A Triangle for Adaora: An African
Book of Shapes* and *Saying Farewell: A Special Goodbye to Mama Nkwelle.*

Ifeoma Onyefulu lives with her two sons in North London.

For His Honour Mr Justice Gideon Quaye and Dorothy

First published in Great Britain in 2003 by Frances Lincoln Limited,
4 Torriano Mews, Torriano Avenue, London NW5 2RZ
www.franceslincoln.com

First paperback edition 2004

British Library Cataloguing in Publication Data available on request

ISBN 0-7112-1938-9 hardback
ISBN 0-7112-2049-2 paperback

Set in Stempel Schneidler

Printed in Singapore

1 3 5 7 9 8 6 4 2

Welcome Dede!

An African Naming Ceremony

IFEOMA ONYEFULU

FRANCES LINCOLN

Introduction

In Africa, a name can tell you a lot about a person: where they come from, what their tribe, extended family or clan is, the day of the week when they were born – even the circumstances surrounding their birth.

My parents waited a long time for me to arrive, so they named me Ifeoma, which means "something good". The name Ifeoma also says that I come from the Ibo tribe of Anambra State, in south-eastern Nigeria.

This story is set among the Ga people of Ghana, where the names Amartai, Amarkai and Amarlai indicate which sons they are in the family – second, third and fifth.

Names are far too important to be left in the hands of young people, so in most parts of Africa grandfathers or older relatives choose the baby's name. But the chief, who is head of the clan, has the final say over the choice of name.

Children in Africa belong not just to their parents, but to the entire clan. Naming ceremonies may vary from area to area, but the idea behind them remains the same. They provide an opportunity for the clan to welcome a baby who, in years to come, will be expected to take a role in the community – as part of a whole new generation.

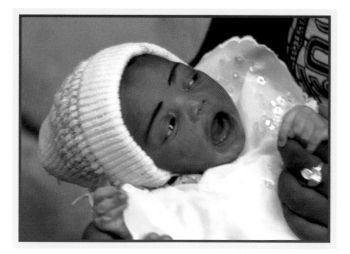

I have a new cousin.
At the moment everyone
calls her "Baby".
   I can't wait for her to have
a name. My name is Amarlai,
and it sounds much nicer
than "Baby".

When I told my uncle, he smiled and said, "You're right, Amarlai. But don't worry – your cousin will soon have a name."

Then he told me about names. "A name is not something you give out like sweets," he said. "It is something you carry all through your life and it tells you a lot about a person: whether they are the first son or daughter, or the second, or the fifth. A name also tells you where a person comes from. So it must be chosen very carefully!"

My name, Amarlai, means I am the fifth son, and my uncle's name, Amarkai, means he is the third son.

My mother's name, Ayeley, means she is the first daughter.
My father's name, Amartai, means he is the second son.

My aunt's name, Ayikai, means she is the third daughter. But when I think about my aunt Ayikai, I don't think about her name – I think about the lovely biscuits she gives me every time she visits us!

Uncle Amarkai also told me that a child has to be eight days old before he or she is given a name. I said, "Eight days? That's a very long time not to have a name!"

 Don't worry, Amarlai," said Uncle Amarkai. "Your grandfather is going to the Chief's house, to ask him if he has chosen the right name. If the Chief says yes, Baby will have a naming ceremony where she will be given her new name."

Yesterday Grandfather and one of my aunts went to see the Chief, and he said the name they had chosen was the right one.

I am so happy! My baby cousin is going to have a naming ceremony. Everyone will be told her name and she will see them all for the first time.

The Chief is head of the family. He is chosen for his wisdom and is expected to carry out a number of duties for the family.

Soon, everyone was running around doing things. One of my aunts went to Central Market to buy food for the naming ceremony. Uncle Amarkai went to get chairs and some corn wine.

Aunt Kai cooked *kenke*, my favourite food, in a big pot. Here she is, stirring the pot on the fire.

Kenke is a savoury ball made with corn. It is ground and left to ferment, then wrapped in leaves and cooked for a few hours.

Three of my aunts wrapped up the kenke in corn skins. Then they put them in a big pan, ready for cooking again.

Here they are, working as hard and as fast as soldier ants!

Yesterday everyone came to Grandfather's house early. The sun was still asleep in the sky. They all said they had come to see my new baby cousin. I was so happy – soon nobody will call her "Baby" any more!

Grandfather shook hands and thanked them all for coming. Then he said, "We are here to welcome our baby into the world. May God bless her!"

Just then, one of my aunts brought Baby for everyone to see.

My aunt is a singer and she is going to help look after Baby until she grows up. Everyone hopes my little cousin will have her gift for singing. And they all said what a lovely baby Baby was.

But Baby spoilt everything by crying!

The baby's mother is not here. She stays at home until her friends and relatives come to tell her that the naming ceremony is over. Even the baby's father does not take part in the naming ceremony.

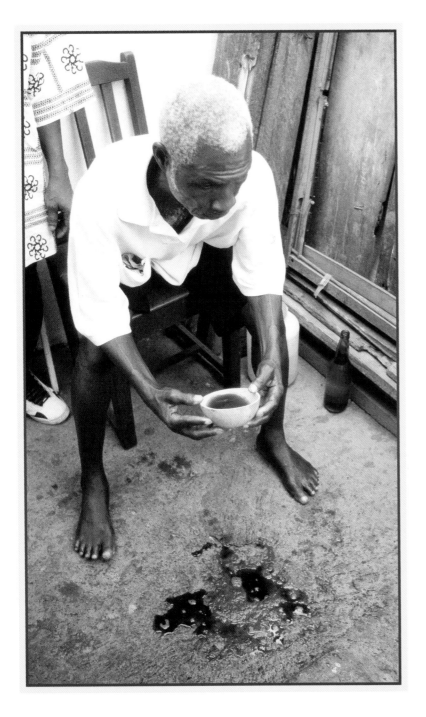

Grandfather said a prayer. He poured some corn wine on the floor to bless the house and everyone in it, then drank a little of the wine.

Corn wine, drunk from a gourd, is traditionally used at Ga ceremonies to help create a harmonious link with family ancestors.

He gave the corn wine to Uncle Tetteh, who passed it to my other uncle. He said some more prayers for Baby and for everyone else, then poured wine on the floor, just like Grandfather, before drinking.

After that, Grandfather dipped his finger in the wine and dropped a tiny bit on Baby's tongue. He said to my little cousin, "Your name is Dede."

Everyone shouted, "DEDE! DEDE!"

Dede means 'The first daughter'.

But Dede was not listening. She was too busy crying. She cried so much, her tiny voice sounded like my cat when he's hungry.

Grandmother's aunt carried Dede home as fast as lightning to see her mother. When she got there, Dede was still crying!

At the end of the naming ceremony the baby's mother comes out to join in the celebrations.

Now it was time to give Dede her presents. First, some people gave her money and everyone clapped their hands. Then someone gave her beautiful cloths.

Another person gave her baby powder, soap, towel and lotion, with a pretty bangle and a beaded necklace for her mother.

Someone else presented her with cans of drinks and a big bag of rice.

Then Grandmother and my aunts offered everyone kenke, to say "thank you".

After that, some of the women ran to tell Dede's mother what had happened at the naming ceremony. Here they are, on their way.

Uncle Amarkai says that in a few days' time there's going to be a party. This time there will be music and dancing for anyone who could not come to the naming ceremony.

And Uncle Amarkai was right! One night, when everything was quiet, I heard loud music and I saw people dancing in the street. There were lots of children, too. They danced until morning!

Now I am very happy that my baby cousin isn't called "Baby" any more.

HER NAME IS DEDE!